GALILE

by Ned Balbo

Ned Balbo

8/6/98
Saratoga Springs,
N.Y.

For Dave Prentiss,

The only man I've ever met who's more compulsive than myself ! Your unassailable logic was one of Saratoga's bright spots. From your poet-in-residence, Ned

Washington Writers' Publishing House
Washington, D.C.

ACKNOWLEDGMENTS
My thanks to the editors of publications in which some
poems first appeared or are forthcoming: *Antioch Review*:
"Late August Light"; *The Cape Rock*: "Whose Son, Whose
Daughter"; *Carolina Quarterly*: "Children Threatened by a
Nightingale"; *The Formalist*: "The Death of Joyce Kilmer,"
"Chesterfield"; *Four Quarters*: "Legacy," "The Stairway Down
to the Sea"; *Kansas Quarterly*: "A Villanelle"; *Möbius*:
"Arrival"; *New CollAge*: "Home for Girls, Long Island"; *Poetry
Baltimore* (WordHouse): "In the Shadow of the Belvedere
Hotel"; *Yankee*: "Blackberries."

Thanks also to the Maryland State Arts Council, and to
James Galvin, David St. John, and Nancy Willard for their
encouragement.

I want to extend special gratitude to Barri Armitage, Arthur
Evenchik, Bill Gifford, Judith Hall, Barney Kirby, and Jane
Satterfield for their support and patience.

Publication of this book is possible thanks to donations
from the many Friends of Washington Writers' Publishing
House.

Cover design by Lynn Springer/DL Graphics Studio

Library of Congress Cataloging-in-Publication Data
Balbo, Ned, 1959–
    Galileo's banquet / by Ned Balbo.
        p.   cm.
    ISBN 0-931846-52-8 (alk. paper)
    I. Title
PS3552.A4454G35   1998
811'.54—dc21   98-12285
                                                          CIP

WASHINGTON WRITERS' PUBLISHING HOUSE P.O. Box 15271 Washington, D.C. 20003

CONTENTS

IV

LOSING OURSELVES

We scatter home at quitting time, the lights
Of streetlamps coming on just now as if
To guide, or warn us. Step back. Suddenly,
Our lives take on a clarity: a door
So much like ours flares gold above these streets
Of ice-chunks, winter-dusk, everything gray
Except the light: the neon twists, the signs,
Locked stores, and headlights. On some other day
I wouldn't even be here. Look, the pines,
Parked cars, the sidewalks, and whatever grief
Hides in these houses—nothing I can see
(As I search past the rooftops, row on row
Of windows set afire, or doors ajar)
Lets out much light against the blackened snow.

This moment won't last long. Soon other lives
Will cross, forsaking solitude, and fuse,
Framed by the light—glimpse of interior,
Ignited lamp—the doorway fans its color
Toward clumped leaves and snowbanks. Do they kiss?—
The door, pushed forward, slams shut. Could I choose
To walk in any door, taking a place
Unnoticed, or else wait till someone leaves,
Slip in and try to blend in with the rest?
Not likely.
            But how would it feel to be
Not one far from his true home, nor one lost
Past all hope, as the first stars of a sky
Deep blue-to-blackening, return at last
To shine as if they'd never been away?

I

To shine is to be surrounded by the dark...
—Donald Justice

ECLIPSE

Outside, stargazers wander on the lawn
In cool metallic light, sunglasses on,
Holding up sheets of cardboard, while the star
Above them dims, the shadow of the moon
Doing what was foretold. This afternoon,
A stone's throw from the Green Earth health food store,
A young man—twenties, with a ponytail—
Stares straight into the slot carved in a box
He lowers now, disappointed, while his friend
Smiles back and shrugs. Shouldn't somebody tell
Them not to give up yet?
                              And here, where looks
Have led to touch, and more, I feel your hand
Against my neck and hair, smooth circles, small
Tense flashings—I can hardly speak at all.

GALILEO'S BANQUET, SIRTURI'S BLISS

At the end of March, 1611, Galileo went to Rome to
induce the ecclesiastical authorities to look through his
telescope. On April 14, 1611, he was invited to an
important banquet...

—Henry King, *The History of the Telescope*

The banquet held in Galileo's honor
Began at sunset when we all took turns
Recovering each word of an inscription
Carved above a door a mile away.
Amazed, we feasted. Rising after dinner,
We stood in line again to see the burns
That marred the moon's thin crescent, and the sky
Grew darker still, dense clusters of small stars
Becoming visible, as if the sun
Had touched them with its light before it fled.
I stepped aside, glanced down and saw small fires
Burning below, through trees. I ate some bread.
A clear night without clouds—the ideal weather.
We did not gladly yield our places, either.

"This we shall call a *telescope*," declared
Prince Frederick, our host. I was impressed
Till I discovered that another man—
The poet Demisiani—had coined the word.
How typical. (I'd learned this from Lagalla
In his justly famous *Lunar Phenomena*,
Not from the gossip of some other guest.)
On the night that he unveiled his invention—
Once we'd had our fill of Jupiter,
All four of its satellites, and each star
The Prince named for himself—Galileo
Dismantled his creation. The moon's advance
Across the sky at last had brought it low—
I waited for my turn to hold the lens.

6

RED PLANET

Overnight Mars will become the playground of the solar system...
—LIFE, May '91

Our choices are endless. Take, for instance,
Mars—
      Long burned-out
beach without an ocean where
light gravity invites tall leaps
past canyons, over cliffs—*And that's just
fine*, you think as you soar toward
the midpoint of your arc and peer out
from your pressure-suit as you imagine
owning a world bereft
of waterfalls and rivers, a world where
red dust glitters down
from glazed plateaus...

Yes, it's beautiful, you think—
The station's slanting into sight; you know now
that you'll soon be home, you'll let
your loved one knead your shoulders
while the lava geysers rise in white-gold
bursts on the horizon, vast drills
tearing through the dried crust, spiralling
downward to the core—*Yes, we could
surely have it all*—you steady your boots
on your descent, knowing well
when nightfall comes, you'll land
and hurry back to base before
the temperature-fall freeze-dries you—
pink dust swirls up toward the stars—
                  And in
the shadow of boiling vats, you touch down

on the pitted landscape, quarry scars
and tire tracks, glancing once more
at the horizon—*There*,
where once a blue gem floated,
and our need was merciless—*Yes, there*—

where one red speck still cuts
across the sky.

CHILDREN THREATENED
BY A NIGHTINGALE

After Max Ernst (oil on wood with wood construction)

No one enters through the arch
at the courtyard's edge.
The nightingale stills his fall, and hovers
over a girl on the grass.

She lies still, crumpled in her nightdress.
The songbird teases down.
Before he attacks again, another girl
runs from the house. Shouting
now, she swings the knife—
The nightingale pulls back into the sky.

But there's another danger: the man
who slips into the house and carries you,
third, youngest girl,
up to the roof; and just before he leaps,
you glance back only once,
your sisters below now smaller, two
who cannot know this flight,
this weightlessness—
                    And you're safe
in a stranger's arms. His palms
balance and press you close.
Somewhere above, a black star
sharpens, and falls.

RANDALL AND WELDON IN NEW YORK

I've seen something of Randall Jarrell lately.
He is rather oddly childish at times: once, in a
restaurant, he became abnormally tickled over
one item on the menu, "Turkey Wing Au Jus"...
—Weldon Kees, July 23, 1946

Heads bowed as if in prayer
above club sandwiches and beer,
the crowd consumes its lunch.
One of two men looks up, laughing.
"Turkey Wing *Au Jus?* Well, after
all, this is a *luncheonette—*
Dear friend, prepare to dine!"
he crows and claps the menu shut.

But Weldon will indulge him—
heads have turned back toward their meals—
for Randall likes his poems "a *lot*"
and doesn't like just anyone's; so Weldon
sips his Coke, grinning at lines
exhumed from cruel reviews: "His poems
sound banged out on a typewriter—
and *by* one." Weldon nods—talk turns
to fairy tales and Freud, new films,
and more, despite missteps: the painters
Weldon praises whom Randall "*abhors...*"

Beyond plate glass and painted letters,
a woman tugs a terrier's leash.

And when, at last, the two men leave,
they pass into the crowd, still smiling,
parting at the corner. Randall
jumps back from the cab—

                         "Thumped
to the roadside like a cat!" he might have cried
if he had known, words caught
by no one within hearing—none but Weldon
who'd wave back, still grinning,
crossing against the light, Weldon
who'd pick his way through traffic,
only nine years left to bring him
to that moment:
                         his car abandoned, mud-splashed
under the Golden Gate, ignition keys
dangling in shadow; black phone
ringing to no avail; a lone cat
pawing at the drapes, printing
its path on the piano—
                         Weldon's blues
sketched out and plotted on the staff.

CLOSING TIME

For R.C.

With Dixie cups of whiskey at our lips,
We'd sip and watch: white neon letters hissed
Above the deli counter where you worked—
Your "base of operations" this late hour.
You called your bookies. Someone swept the floor
While you took all the risks, weighing how much
To "borrow" from the register, how soon
To pay it back before the owner guessed
What grand scheme you pursued. Away at school
You kept up the performance, drank and brawled
Until you lost your scholarship for good,
And sulked back home, another wastrel son
Condemned to count out change. Your luck had turned.
Drunk-driving home one night, you crashed and burned.

What happened? *You were late, all bets were down...*
But I remember you, an expert's touch
That tore through sheets of tinfoil, then sliced off
Large clumps of bread, cold meat as metal clacked
Against the board, grinning as you stood there
Talking about your "friends"—the boy who wore
One false eye carved from wood, the girl who lurked
Far from the dance floor propped up on a stiff,
Quite unconvincing wooden leg, sad child
Who longed to dance but knew she never would;
And when they met...
                But that's another tale,
Except to say they failed—like us, perhaps—
To find their own affliction mirrored in
One whom no odds would favor or protect.

GRISSOM WAY

Hauppauge, New York

Virgil "Gus" Grissom was among the Apollo 1 astronauts
who died during a preflight test, January 27, 1967

A right off 111—Wheeler Road,
It's called along this stretch—and now I'm driving
Onto Grissom Way, a street named for
      The astronaut—who else? It has to be—

The road ahead curves forward, falls away.
This world's serene: parked cars and window boxes
Flooded with carnations, evergreens
      And hedges marking out the properties—

Split-levels, ranches—close to Orbit Lane.
What names! A pinwheel spins among azaleas
As I press the brake, better to look
      For signs of life. Slow down. But who lives here

      Where past and future meet, boarding that camper—
Yes, a Pioneer—for parts unknown
Soon as the summer comes? What family's learned
      To tolerate that Rambler propped on blocks,

      Never to be restored? I ease the pedal,
Glance to the left. A man in shirt and tie
Inspects his bushes, kneeling—back from work,
      About to leave? I turn as he recedes,

And someone else appears: she shuts her mailbox—
Bright red mini-barn—then pauses, head down,
Leafing through letters as I watch the world
      slide by, safe beyond glass, unreachable.

Atlantic Place—but weren't our ships dispatched
To the Pacific, choppers sent ahead
While radar swept the sky? I check the mirror:
    Yes, a '58 or '59,

    Same age as Project Mercury, two more
Before Gregarin/Shepard, lost from view,
Made history, and Virgil Grissom, too,
    Broke through the outer reaches, soon to plunge

    Into the sea, waves closing on his craft...
It's Telstar Lane—a dead end—as I turn
The steering wheel and find myself on course—
    Late forsythia, stray cat, hockey net

Abandoned on a sidewalk. Now a glimpse
Of Spacecraft Lane: tree-shaded like the rest
Of them, bleached shingles, and at apogee
    The sun above bright homes soon to be sold,

    Century 21, the realtor's claim
Staked out on several lawns. I tap the brake,
Try for a better look; the street slopes down
    Ahead, gently at first. Near someone's pool

    Clear water kicks up over redwood walls,
Door-slams, smell of chlorine. Homes sold, re-sold
Until we end up circling, lost again
    On streets vaguely familiar, still surprised

    To find the world transformed, ourselves displaced—
You know the rest. I glance up at the sign:
Apallo Lane (misspelled). Carpenter Lane:
    Another astronaut. Or Wheeler Road,

Named for someone who must have been well known—
What did he build, discover, or explore?
Light slides across clear glass. On Grissom Way,
    I close the circle past a Grand Marquis

    Parked on a driveway, maple-leafed in shadow,
Plum-red, new paint gleaming as the street
Fades fast, and I speed up, letters impressed
    In metal meant to last, "Gus" Grissom's name

    Behind me now, the fire that took his life
And White's, and Chafee's, one more tragedy
Now swept away. And all that I can see
    Ahead of me shines brightly, far away.

BLACKBERRIES

Late July. So few
are left among the leaves...
Finally, their soft flesh
streaks the clear walls of the jar.
Stars flare on above the trees, fires
that tear the shreds of clouds.
The cedar bends its neck and sways.
Crickets know. There's a break in their singing.
But when you stand, legs nicked with blood,
the world has changed:
A porch lamp flickers above the house,
night birds scatter against stone pines—
their only sign, the fall of needles—
and the dark earth turns its shoulder.
So is there anything to trust
besides the cool jar that you hold,
these black gems soft and full of juice,
this fruit like tiny worlds, all one,
now in your mouth?

II

Whoever you are,
Who may have made some kind gesture
To me on my earth, you are welcome
To me and mine.

—James Wright

APOLLO

July 20, 1969

You shook me once, "It's happening." Awake
In blue light while my father, fast asleep,
Sprawled on the floor, head buried in a pillow,
I blinked up at the screen, the lunar module
Breaking away to fall off into space
Down to the moon. But how long would it take,
How many hours? I stared but could not keep
From nodding off, white swirls of flame, those hollow
Voices chewed by static while the pale,
Scarred surface shone below. "We've won the race,"
You said, spooning a pear-slice from the dish
Propped on your lap as I, too, broke away,
Falling back into darkness, weightless, flash
Of light sent floating, freed of memory.

CHILDLESS IN A TIME OF PLENTY

For my adoptive parents, Carmine and Elizabeth;
ca. 1949–1959

In that first year, past thirty, married late,
You'd lie with her all afternoon while smoke
Broke at the ceiling and the cigarette
You shared burned down to ashes. You would run
One finger along her scar—how long it took
To heal, the baby torn from her—"Stop it,"
A pause; and all was well again. The fan
Clattered and shook the house, a constant note

That, swirling, helped you sleep—"We'll have a child,
Who knows, miracles happen"—waking, chilled,
Resigned to the day's labors. How many times
Just home from work, you heard, scrubbing your hands,
False proofs of pregnancy, omens or symptoms
You, too, hoped were real? On weekends—

Well, Sundays, your one day off—you'd run the mower
Across your quarter acre, blast the shower
Across your back and shave fast to emerge
Prepared for Mass, her family's scrutiny,
Dressed in the clothes she'd chosen. Or she'd cry,
Daughter and mother silenced by some charge
Held close to the heart for decades, powers of ten
Concealed yet multiplied, much as the dime

Slipped beneath Saint Teresa's pedestal
Was thought to call down luck, winged Mercury
With rumors of good fortune... Soon you'd fly
Together in your Pontiac, slow down
Close to the car lots, when you had the time,
And watch for the new Buicks waxed to flash

Their curves in light or dusk. Summers would end;
Childless, you'd watch night fall. And when you'd wish
One of the children wheeling past were yours
(Faint squeal of pedals, bells; slow, passing cars
That scattered them), as if by chance you'd rest
One hand against her thigh then let it fall
After a moment, until she stood up,
As if uncomfortable against the step,

And turned, "Time to go in?"...*The years go fast,*
And when they bear us to a place we've long
Imagined, we may well retrace each wound
Without remorse; even, perhaps, with love.
But when those years are gone?... You watched her move,
And in that moment nothing could go wrong.

ELIZABETH AND ELAINE

Summer, 1967

I shook off the drops, and looked for my mother.
Elizabeth, glancing toward the deep end of the pool,
edged close to her younger sister. Elaine kicked water,
dangling her feet. Lance swam past, split the sun
in two, as Elizabeth laughed and shouted, "Dive!"—
tossing up coins. Blue sky, reflected clouds

that shattered instantly. I kicked through clouds
still rumbling, but Lance was older, faster. Our mothers
watched us streaming with water from our dives.
Elizabeth's jaw drew tight—this was *her* pool.
Lance offered the coins; she took them. Would her son
surface just once, fists filled with coins, not water?

"Go!" She threw them to my side of the water.
I shot from the chrome steps, swam as if clouds
broke open inside my lungs, a dozen suns
sparkling before my eyes. I headed toward mother-
of pearl, vision blurred, polished floor of a pool
still spattered with change, falling short as I dived

for nothing—a coin or two. Lance rose, every dive
triumphant. Elizabeth stared at the water,
waves displaced by his weight. I was tired of the pool.
Elaine twisted the strap of her suit, face clouded,
her sister circling tensely—*I'm his mother*—
Elaine looked away, caught watching her sons,

first Lance, then me: *How could I give him away?* The sun
touched her bright hair, almost dry...Only one more dive,
one chance to prove who was the better mother.
I gulped air; the light dimmed, shadow crossing the water
where loose change, falling, glittered through clouds
that scattered as all turned calm...The clear light of the pool

exploded. Submerged, I looked up: just a game of pool,
Lance banking from wall to wall, the firstborn son
slammed his fist on my chest, reached further through clouds
that tore as I choked and surfaced. Another failed dive.
I coughed, fought back tears, and dropped underwater—
Elaine whispered, "When will you tell him I'm his mother?"—

as I bounced, weightless in silence. A mother's
face rippled—I didn't want to come up, or breathe—and a cloud
of gnats touched the surface of the water.

AZALEA COURT, 1958–1962

For Elaine

"This baby's mine. I'll raise her when she's born,"
And here on the back porch, screened-in under sunlight
Threaded along the trellis, it's a vow
You know you'll never break. You're twenty-one,
Your unborn daughter isn't his, and so
You've fled from your own home—or was it his—
Back here, to your mother's house. The son you bore
Him, Lance, scatters toys across cold cement—

And now you hear your mother shouting through
The faucet-bursts, *You should have, should have, should have*
Breaking through the clatter of the plates,
And shut your eyes into a memory—
Pick one—that soothes, where bells ring past the roofs
Of scrubbed, Between-War houses. Nothing moves...

≈

A neighbor's radio—smooth voice and lush strings—
What *isn't* in bloom? But here pigs' feet
Spit from the skillet that your mother holds.
"Come in and eat," she calls, and so you rise,
Not yet humbled enough. She lifts your son
Out of your arms. Sit down. Don't say a word—
"*Mother...*" You realize you *are* that word—

And scraping the bowl this woman wields the spoon
And waves you off. The baby grasps at air,
Propped in his high chair. Then, speaking as if
Without a thought, "He called today. One word,
And I knew he was drunk again, or worse.
He swears he'll never give you the divorce."

Outside, the pear's gold fruit is ripening.

~

Cicadas, clacking fan, the crossing bells—
You just can't get to sleep. Your daughter kicks,
Due any day now, restless. Tired of heat,
These pains, this heaviness, of being too young
To take your son and flee—where would you *go?*—
You can't even imagine all the choices
Now to be foreclosed. And so, these nights
You wander out, hoping to clear your head,
Remembering Don, your lover, in a glaze
Of Christmas lights that shone along the gutters
Of the house while snow erased the lawn.
You kissed—
                And now that same ground's glistening
Under your feet. You kneel and touch fine strands
Of dew that break when taken in your hands.

~

You gave your baby daughter to Don's mother,
Careful to protect the custody
Of Lance, your son. Your husband never knew,
But asked forgiveness, begged, or threatened you
For four years till he finally set you free.
Too late. By then, you'd had a second son—
Same lover, Don again—as if once more,
With luck, you two might get the timing right.
You didn't, forfeiting the second child
You'd conceived together...
                              What better way
To say it all, in bold strokes—that you'd gain
Your freedom back at any cost in scandal,
Grief, and human wreckage?
                              Even I,
That second child you gave up, would concede.

—Oh, would you? You can't know what it was like,
Divorced at last, yet forced to keep my word—
As if I'd had a choice back in those days
When scandal was kept secret. Yes, it hurt
Each time we gathered to play out our roles—
And so carved flesh fell into place, in Mother's
House amid the gravy-fumes and small talk
Strained to bursting where the daughter whom
I dared not call mine ducked under the table
To be coaxed out not by her own father
Standing right there, nor by me but her—
My mother-in-law-to-be purring in German,
Schatzi, *while you bounced on Elizabeth's lap,*
Son I dared ask to hold—
                              How could you know?

DESCENT

For Elizabeth, April 1973

What was it marked the ceiling the day you told
me I wasn't yours, I was your sister's child...
You touched your eyes.
                    I stared into the floor,
sunlit linoleum, gold swirls and stars...Your voice
choked up and cracked—
                    All sound had turned to noise—
the ticking of pipes, of clocks; what then? I know
I tore the covers down and then lay quiet...
You passed by in the hall, your face was wet.
I saw—or did I?—the dusk-glow of the hall
beyond my room; faint rattlings or no sound
outside my room? Cracked photos, many shelves
of figurines wiped clean—
                    And tumbling from the bars
of its cage, our finch leapt wildly for hours.

A NEW START

For Elizabeth; Brentwood, New York, 1967

"Wait here." You strode across the lawn, black salt-
And-pepper hair, black skirt, your high-heeled shoes
Stabbing the grass while I sat at the fence,
Split-rail beneath the maple. "Anyone home?"
You called out once again, as if by circling
Round the yard, weaving through shrub and rose-
Beds, tapping windows, you'd *make* them appear.
The sun beat down. This house would soon be ours
And so much would be solved when we moved in—
Old neighbors you'd pulled close too suddenly,
The long feuds afterward—all these erased
When we moved "one last time": a new start, maybe,
One more second chance...You passed the sign
Staked on the lawn, snapping aside a branch,
White birch left to grow wild, then disappeared
Around the house, dirt-brown split-level ranch
Two blocks from your new friend. And who was *she*,
"Aunt" Elfie, who'd searched out this house for sale—
Mother of *Schatzi*, freshly dyed flame-hair—
Pouring herself the drinks that you refused?
All night, shaking ourselves to rock 'n' roll,
Her daughter and I danced to old 45s
Down in that panelled basement while the men
Laughed over shots of whiskey, needle scraping
When we thumped too hard...Where were you now?
A bird, black silhouette, veered toward the power
Lines, grabbed hold of the clumped knot stretching toward
A stripped pole near the woods. A motor gunned,
And in the distance children's—strangers'—cries.
I didn't want to move, and yet I did—
*If you were right, this time...*I liked the daughter—
What would I have noticed? How she laughed
In shrieks, almost; how long you'd watched us both,
Till on the drive home you'd leaned close to say,

Quietly, to my father, it was *good*—
Good that we'd know each other growing up.
What could you mean? I pushed the thought away—
But on that day, mid-June, trapped in a yard
Flooded with light, breaking apart the seeds
That fluttered down, I heard your voice again
Greeting the car. You clasped the owner's hands
As she emerged, caught off-guard while the door
Thumped shut, her husband from the driver's side
Crossing to greet you as she stepped away
Stiffly. The closing loomed; more paperwork,
But why had we come *really*? To see *friends*—
Strangers we hardly knew—who'd disappear,
The deal complete, into their separate lives
As anyone but you would understand,
Smiling too widely, talking through their nods
And curt replies, praising your new best friend,
Her daughter, all the luck that brought you here,
Certain at last you'd find yourself betrayed
No longer, that you'd fled the past for good
Here in a world remade. You called my name—
But what if you were right?—and I obeyed.

WHOSE SON, WHOSE DAUGHTER

For Kim ("Schatzi"), ca. 1975

Sister, when you blew smoke against the glass,
I looked up at the school bus, stood below
In snow. For months you knew whose son I was,

Whose daughter you were. A block away, your house,
Grandparents who'd raised you, waited. Crunching snow,
The bus moved on. You blew smoke on the glass.

Red stoplights flashed, brakes groaned again. Your voice
Carried as you stepped off. Don't look back now—
For months before I knew whose son I was,

We'd pass in the halls then look away. I guess
When told, you thought, *It's better not to know.*
I watched. Laughing, you'd blown smoke on the glass

While I imagined other lives for us,
Those missing years. If I'd been raised with you—
All gone. I thought I'd known whose son I was,

But now...Too late. You'd passed from view. The bus
Scattered exhaust on snow heaped by the plow.
How much was lost, like breath against cold glass...
You tried hard to forget whose son I was.

LATE AUGUST LIGHT

In memory of Elizabeth, 1916–1977

White radish, mint and spinach
push the earth aside.
You hoe the ground as if lost in thought,
your forehead smudged.
In the next yard, maple seeds
come loose, spilling
their soft words to the lawn.

Strung up, the paws of rabbits
dangle in the shade.

An old man turns toward a cave of leaves.
Our neighbor under the maple-light
flickers, then walks back into our world,
holding them up: fur cleansed with light,
a curve of nails.

I watch from the patio,
trimming the tall grass at its edge.
We pretend we haven't seen him.
You lose yourself in the clink of stones.
The blade scrapes into the soil, sinks,
and for a while I hear only
the sound of shears—

till, coming awake, I hear the voices
lost in the long yard's distance:
a woman's (yours), an old man's mingling
as your laughter nears the fence.

The charm he's called you to receive
revolves, suspended above the rails.

Late August light arrests the leaves, now motionless.

CHESTERFIELD

The brand my mother smoked was Chesterfield
While talking to my father or the phone.
A flared match to the tip, clouds broke apart,
Or puffed out when she spoke. It was an art,
Like any skill, once mastered. When she held
Her prop, imagined elegance infused
Her every gesture lifted from old films
That mesmerized her during the Depression,
Shot "in glorious black-and-white," sleek realms
Of men tragically distant, yet amused
By their own irony; pale heroines
Who wept or else leaned backward to be kissed;
Families with secret griefs, or public sins
Good wives endure...A slow dissolve, to mist.

HOME FOR GIRLS, LONG ISLAND

Elizabeth, ca. 1929

They've got someone's attention, finally:
Photographer unknown, this mob of girls
In dresses bleached to near-transparency
Squeezes before the lens, set free to smile—
All faded, water-stained over the years.
Who brought them here, to this Victorian house
Built on bare land, dune-drifts, clumps of weed,
Or just bad soil? Is this their residence?

And you, too: starched and scoured with the rest—
Cleansed, almost—still astonished when you think
Of all that changed the day you choked back tears,
Struggling to tell who hit you, held you down
Beneath his weight. When blows began to fall
Before you'd finished speaking, how surprised—
And yet, beyond surprise—you found yourself,
Past all thought she would pull you close again...

—And yet, each time she visits, you forgive
Your mother, waiting to be taken home.

III

And learn, with joy, the gulf, the vast, the deep.
—Louise Bogan

SOLDIERS OF CHRIST

Before Confirmation, April 1971

You may know this already—I did not—
But when a man is nailed to a cross,
His full weight on his wrists and arms, each shoulder
Pulling him back down, it isn't loss
Of blood from wounds that proves the greatest threat
To his survival, nor the need for water
Worse as he sweats, nor hunger, nor exposure
Though all these increase with every hour.
What kills fastest is the need for air:
To breathe, somehow, though as his chest is torn
Still further from his diaphragm, each breath
Grows shallower the more hard-fought, his poor
Flesh bent and drawn taut as when we are born.
Not breathing, finally, is the cause of death.

True, it's always been a *sign*...And yet,
Not once during those three days did we hear
What broke His human frame and made Him fall.
Instead, we prayed, excused from public school
By order of the parish, drilled in doctrine,
Marched to church and taught to kneel and wait,
Head bowed, for the bishop's blow, our hearts on fire
For some kind priest to let us out again.
"Soldiers of Christ," and drafted all too soon,
We smirked, yet still saw all things through a prism
Of stained glass and years of catechism
Even the real soldiers we'd seen perish
All our lives on newscasts, whose poor flesh,
Seared or shot down, looked frail, like our own.

IN THE SHADOW OF THE BELVEDERE HOTEL

Before the Gulf War, Baltimore, 1990

Framed by the news box window, the boy
holds on to his girl. She stares forward,
eyes wet under a cap
of desert camouflage. Soon,
she'll have to give it back.

I'm in the shadow of the Hotel Belvedere,
downtown, Charles and Chase, where lions
snarl from the mansard roof, carved owls
prepare to strike, and people crowd
at the bus stop, or push by.

In months to come, this girl will learn
to live without the boy, wine poured, forgotten,
warm in a glass, while black wings
fill the sky with sound. And that boy
with the cropped mustache and bare scalp
visible through bristles
will pass the weeks in trenches, pale sand
spilling over dunes—more thunder,
and all the stars that, flashing, cross and rise...

Sentimental? Maybe. But that's why
we buy the news—a pigeon
wobbles along the ledge, no bus
looms forward, out of traffic—and still
the revolving door keeps spinning,
spits out men in suits whose hands
glide down the smooth, brass bannisters.
Quartet of columns, quoins and cornices,
the Belvedere by day is beautiful...

And tonight, when I pass under bright letters
sharp and pseudo-Gothic, each one

traced along stem and serif with neon
tubes that burn white-hot, to feel
myself rise toward the roof in a mirrored box
gilt-edged and gleaming, I'll walk out
onto the thirteenth floor, lounge filled
with smoke and a keyboard's clang, flat crooning
through synthetic trumpets. A woman in silk
will slide onto her man; laughing, he'll reach
under her dress—
            And though I know
this hotel's bankrupt, the lounge to be closed
the first of the year, I'll drink, glance down
at the lights that float beyond north and south walls
made of glass. I'll see the Monument
lit from the ground, the Domino Sugars sign
in neon, red stars
flashing on unseen planes, rooftop lights
that never go out—

like some boy who peers at fireworks glittering.

STARS VISIBLE

Vanderbilt Planetarium, Centerport, Long Island

Banquet of constellations, when you rise
And sweep across the sky, I'll know your stars
From visits to the planetarium:
Knees clenched, head back, I'd gaze up while the gold
Lights broke the darkness, and a man's voice boomed
From speakers wracked with static. Then a flash:
North Pole and Northern Lights, convenient tags
To mark locations at the Arctic's edge,
Ice-cliffs along the sky's circumference
Surrounding us. Gears whirred. And then the fires
That pricked the blue-black ceiling disappeared.
I took a breath; but new configurations—
Stars of another hemisphere, lost gods,
Crustacean-claws, dead heroes—rose instead.

A VILLANELLE

I gently say, "You are my villanelle,"
Some morning nonsense meant to make her smile.
Sunlight warms the window as it falls,

Softly, against our faces. She is still
Asleep, it seems. I knock the windowsill
And gently say, "You are my villanelle,"

But she does not respond. As usual,
I am content to wait a little while.
Sunlight warms the window as it falls

Like snow or early rain whose touch reveals
Fine lines around her eyes, invisible
At night. My sleeping poem, my villanelle,

Wake up. Her breathing slows, and on the walls
Faint patterns—shadows—dance their silent roles.
Sunlight warms the window. As it falls,

Eyes closed, she speaks at last, "How could you tell?"
And smiles. No line has ever worked as well
As this one. She repeats, "My villanelle…"
And sunlight warms the window as it falls.

LEGACY

After Herrick

To those
of you
who live:
these cliffs
above
the sea,
black waves;

to those
who die:
belief,
at least
enough
to help
you rest.

For one
who lives
nor dies,
no grave
is deep
enough
for sleep

and love;
my dreams
all hum
like flies—
I'm lost.
So talk:
it's dark.

BRIDES OF FRANKENSTEIN

Elizabeth Frankenstein to her husband;
after James Whale's classic, 1935

Pretorius created men from "seed,"
He said, and women, too—unveiling them
With relish, each no larger than a doll,
Sealed within six glass jars while you looked on,
Astounded by the miniature lives
He showed you one by one—The King and Queen,
The Ballerina who would only dance
To Mendelssohn's *Spring Song*—"A bore," he sighed,
Long jaded by what once was novelty,
Even a kind of genius. *You* would know.
He grimaced, stuffed the King back in his jar,
Replaced each bell-shaped shroud, and set them all
Back in the box—bright-handled, coffin-shaped—
To sit in darkness till next called upon.

And then he called on *you*, downing his gin,
Talked of "collaboration" and the "size"
His own creations lacked, while there you sat,
Spellbound, half-trembling at the thought of what
Together you'd achieve, wild-eyed, a shared
Life's work conceived in darkness, coils flashing
In your salvaged lab. Husband, how could
You not refuse him, as you should have done?
And yet, abandoned for so long the nights
Brought nothing to this bed besides more grief,
I should have known no vow would call you back,
Or wake you to your loss. For you, at last,
All births were one, all lives stitched limb by limb
Into these bodies brought to light again.

ARISTARCHOS AND HIS COSMOS

Aristarchos went even further...The Sun, not the Earth,
was at rest in the centre of the starry sphere. This was basically
the same view that Copernicus, 1700 years later, advocated
in greater detail and with fuller arguments. Aristarchos'
suggestion was not taken very seriously...

—Toulmin and Goodfield, *The Fabric of the Heavens*

I see the daily motion of the stars
And it is all illusion, all a lie.
How easily we find the human eye
May be deceived. It is the earth that moves,
Revolving on its axis. Yes, of course,
And, honored Heraclitus, you're more right
Than even you suspect; for every night
That constellations shift or stars regress
Toward the horizon, fading as they pass,
It's we, not they, who move, dark fact that proves
What I remain still hesitant to voice—
For if they're motionless, could not some force
Propel our own green planet on a course
Around a sun that's also motionless?

This I deduced, and sought to tell the world—
"The cosmos has more grandeur than we thought;
So large it is that by comparison
The orbit of the earth is but a point
Within the vast, starred surface of a sphere—
Look, here's my diagram." But everyone
I called on (former colleagues) looked annoyed
For having stood and wasted half an hour.
One smiled and touched my arm. "You have a point,
But think it through. What stops us being hurled
Together with our houses and our wives,
And all that we possess into the void?"
I wanted to reply but could not yet
Divine the force that binds us to our lives.

THE BOUNDARIES

What exists beyond the universe—
Gold sun burning out among the stars,
White sand on a beach three worlds away,
Blue sky breaking up against the sea
Into a million flashings, broken
Mirrorings where one face, only one
Appears when I look away again—

And past the sky are satellites
That flash and spin. Invisibly,
They pass, like the forgotten lives
That built them in our century—
They fall before undying heat,
Then burn to ash near Mercury

Or else hurl on, off course
Past the boundaries of this verse.

IV

O shooting star
that fell into my eyes and through my body—:
Not to forget you. To endure.

—Rilke

FIRST DAYS IN A WORLD

For Caroline

*Like hearing parents, some deaf parents also expect
to have a child who is the same as themselves...[But
in the case of deaf parents of hearing children,] how
is it possible that parent and child from two such
different worlds can meet?*

        —Paul Preston, *Mother Father Deaf*

Right now, of everything that's visible
And yet means nothing, this shy man, your father
Deaf since birth, who's watched you for an hour,
May be most important. He's been told
His twin daughters, weeks premature, can hear,
But can't believe it yet, not till he sees
Some sign in your response beyond the glass
Dividing him from you. He taps the window,
Sensing its vibration; taps again,
And all the babies twitch. How small your hands
Are, flexing while your sister cries; and now
He knows—elated, saddened—*Time to go,*
The nurse touches his arm, and so he does,
Though when he finds your mother still asleep,
He'll have nowhere to go except the lobby
Or outside, to smoke...For you, whose newborn
Hands, short-fingered, dense with lines, close now
And fall down at your side, the world is what
Rocks you within its hum, all cries except
Your own drowned out, a bright machinery
That warms you in its shell. You want so much
Just to be held these first days in a world
More like his than you'll ever know again.

VERMEER'S EXECUTOR

As it happens, Leeuwenhoek was a poor artist and he
never did any drawings as far as we know. Instead,
he used to show what he was observing to an artist,
and would then check over the results.

⌒

[In 1676, Leeuwenhoek] was asked to sort out the
financial problems left by the death of Vermeer, and in
this way became the great painter's executor.

—Brian Ford, *Single Lens:*
The Story of the Simple Microscope

When I paint, I told him, it's the light
Which fascinates me most—a woman's hand
Lifting an empty balance touched with pearls
Of light; the dull brass and the darker shading;
A string of real pearls tossed on a table;
Gold coins, and her face half-lit by sun
That sifts in through the partly opened window
—These are what interest me. I told him so,
Preparing my regrets, watching the swirls
That float in water drops, the moth-wing's vein,
Blood cells and rotifers, the lifeless mite,
Nodding as I peered through the scrap of metal
Framing the lens that he himself had ground.
"If you would sketch all this with pen and ink—"

I looked down, and declined. He took the dish
Dark green with clumps of algae thick as flesh,
And tipped it toward the center of the sieve,
Then sat there, quite still, watching water fall
Through mesh where small shreds, barely visible,
Clung fast or washed away. "The light is poor,"
He said at last. I brought the candle near,
Still waiting while he brushed aside the haze
That tore and drifted. Finally, I could leave;
Why did I pause?

An artist could do worse
Than to behold a hidden universe,
Sketching it out, under a watchful gaze—

—But, gently then, he touched the verdigris
That stained crossed wire. This universe was his.

THE DEATH OF JOYCE KILMER

For Caroline (her recollection of
Joyce Kilmer Square, South Boston)

You crossed the intersection named for Joyce
For years, and as you turned, each sudden noise—
Each tire-squall, brake-screech, or jammed-on horn—
The silence also, when *it* was the sound—
Remembered her to you. When was she born?
You thought of her last moments. Was the wind
So strong when she took off after the hat
Snatched from her head and tossed across the street

To roll on past the firebox, on its brim?
And even now that you know Joyce is not
A girl, not from South Boston, nor the victim
Of some traffic accident you thought
The Square commemorated, you recall
Her still and cannot un-believe it all.

THE TWIN PROBLEM

—What's that? Of course you know:
We face it all our lives. It's what we glimpse
In mirrors passed in haste, what we become
On blending with the crowd. It's when the sky,
Still blue with sunlight, holds the moon—pearl-white,
Degraded twin that has replaced its sister,

Somehow, or is this a fallen sun
Grown pale and weak? You see the problem. When
Stars rise and multiply, almost the same
Seen by the eye—small planets, satellites,
Red dwarfs or giants—all are points of light
Scattered across the sky, and yet a lens

Reveals new sets of twins: binary stars,
Twin moons, and, yes, those legendary twins,
Founders of ancient Rome who haunt us still,
As do those stellar fish lured far upstream
To nip each other's tailfins. Think of sperm
Released in bursts, swift-moving, as they surge

Toward eggs in swirls of motion, infinite,
Or nearly so, like stars. Can multitudes
Consist of many million pairs of twins?
And what of many eggs, those tiny moons?
Clasped all those months in darkness, Elvis had
A twin, stillborn at birth, "identical"—

Or so it's said, though one of them was dead—
One sperm, one egg that fused then later split,
One bright, one dark. But if both twins survive
Their one shared childhood, coming to rest
Separate at last, alone, in that one moment,
Each will plan the other's violent death

But seldom see it through. Or else they'll seek
Out difference for its own sake: one stands tall,
Well-read, and graceful, one stares at the wall,
Sunk down in vice, the classic Evil Twin.
Now they can glance in mirrors: what looks back
Is not the other but themselves at last.

The problem solved? Not quite. In all of us
A dark one lurks, dead ringer for the self,
Which darkness coaxes from the negative
Where it's immersed into the light again.
Dr. Jekyll and Mr. Hyde—the same.
The werewolf set free by the moon—or is it

The rising sun that frees the man? The same,
And opposites—the Twin Problem again.
It boggles the mind: twins nowhere, everywhere,
All like each other, unlike, all the same,
But never quite; one that is somehow two
And yet still one...If you began again

By saying, *Twins are two who are the same,*
Identical in every way, you'd feel,
Perhaps, that you'd solved something. Think again.
Consider long-lost twins, each seized at birth,
Brought up without the other. Past unknown,
They're secretly observed. Are they still twins

In spirit as in fact? One wears the half-
Coin necklace, family heirloom, broken mirror-
Image of the one her brother wears—
(But mirror-images are never twins,
Are they? They're opposites! That was a test.)—
And when these two halves fuse...?
                                        But what of us,

Platonic souls whose quest will only end
When like two travellers orbiting a star,
We find reunion in the act of love?
Siamese twins? Don't even mention them.
The so-called "mirror stage"? We'll skip that now.
Instead, let us just think about the moon

That makes the tides, pale moon that makes all love
Bear fruit in cycles that are marked by blood,
A spattering of seed, and, later, birth—
Cool sheets on pale skin...Same moon that makes
Me call out to you now, my Twin.
       Say when
We two will fuse under the stars again.

ROOM GONE DARK

For Caroline, and for Charles and Liz Beckman

I kneel at the top of the stairs under the skylight
White with sun and call out to the child
Of married friends. Plucked from the living room
Near-dangerous with toys, he's learned to crawl
Upstairs "all by himself. Just watch, he will,"
His mother vows, laughing. Her palms are black

From crawling with her son. She smooths the black
Wisps of his hair and points him toward the light.
Arms wide, I call his name. She works her will,
Wipes off his face, cajoles him till the child,
Chuckling, unsteadily begins to crawl,
Hands braced against the first step. From the room

Beyond, his father warns, "Just give him room,"
Then joins his wife to cheer him past the black
Scars of the wood, then thump! the baby crawls
In laughter, drool-stained, cooing, each limb light,
So breakable, I fear...I have no child,
Although for years I told myself, *You will*

One day...A foot slips—And, against my will,
Images flood back, these same friends, this room
Where only months before you held their child,
Then almost weightless, rocking him. A black
Lock of your hair slipped down. "But he's so *light*."
You offered, "Want to hold him?"—Past the scrawl

Of wood-grain on the stairs, this long, slow crawl
To glory just half finished, the baby's will
Is fading fast. Now mesmerized by light,
He stares past me, turns back to glimpse the room
He's just abandoned, and explodes in tears, the black
Keys of a toy piano struck and rolled, a child's

Twin mallets clanging on a xylophone, one child
Never to be conceived, never to crawl,
Struggling to stand at last, her hair black
As her mother's, eyes blue, but when will
They darken?...As I lean back to make room,
His father scoops the boy up toward the light

Where he'll crawl in midair past the black-
Framed skylight. And, beyond, in some far room
Gone dark, I'll find you cradling our child.

ST. JAMES, NEW YORK: IN RAINFALL

Elaine, ca. 1994

Hear it? Rain on the roof, just starting out:
The patio is cool and all the leaves
Are shaking with a million small collisions,
Countless accidents. From where I sit
These colors of the yard bleed out as if
This backyard were the painting of a yard
Most brilliant just before it's washed away.
Because it's washed away? I almost wish
It *had* been, but these flowers and vines still touch
The bright grass, while the gutters crack and churn
Their contents to the ground; lit from within,
White birch and silver ash; the maple-line
Along the fence; the fountain with its now
Redundant offering, its splendid cherub...

~

I would have said I saw you yesterday,
But I've been wrong too often. I know now
It's always someone who looks almost like you,
Or as I imagine you, at times
Caught by surprise, in crowds...

> *Kids dare the cars*
By stepping off the curb then jumping back,
The WALK sign flashing as they rush between
Stopped cars and shriek. Laughing, they flood the street
And run past, calling out to friends ahead—
I check the mirror as the light turns green
And, suddenly, you're there—

58

But you'd be older,
Thinner, not so tall; or else I've glimpsed
The child you were and not the man you are
Before you disappear beyond the crosswalk.

~

You've stayed away—what is it? Fifteen years
As if it were some kind of punishment
That Don and I must bear. Or is it more
Like spite, as if nothing we said or did
Would ever matter but those few mistakes
We made when hardly older than you were
When you last cared to visit; we were *kids*,
For heaven's sake, it's time now to forgive

And, yes, forget somehow. Our sons agree—
Your brothers, Shawn and Dean. Could you not want
To know us when we're part of *you* as well?—
And don't you fear that someday you'll return
To find your father dead, myself as well—
What words choked back, crossed off or never said…

~

—Azaleas, tulips, lilacs, all as vivid
As they'll ever be, almost as wet
And all soon to be drowned. None of this matters.
Fresh soil swirls to mud, the roses twitch
Or bend when it rains harder—
                                                    That last time
You looked out on this yard, I told you why
We'd given up your sister and yourself
To separate houses, why we couldn't raise
You as we wished, why once again we sought
Some small place in your lives…You sat right here
And faced me—restless, skeptical, I thought,
The picture of your father in his youth,
Outside the house in which you should have lived,

The house to which your father and our boys
At last return. Door-slams, crackle of bags,
Noises that break apart, as bottles hiss
And shoes clump in the hallway—Silence, rain,
And laughter; other, long-familiar sounds…
The rainstorm ends. Along the nearest branch
Of dogwood, drops of water fall in light
That strikes each bead to fire; one by one,
They stretch, grow heavier then slide away,
A thousand all at once, and everywhere
Around this yard and garden, it's the same:
Each surface streaked with water, struck by light
So blinding it erases what's beneath—

—Why dwell on this? It happened. Bad enough.

THE STAIRWAY DOWN TO THE SEA

For M.W., and for Carmine,
on Father's Day, 1987

My father pokes the mud shark: white sand spills
Out of torn gills.
He drops the branch, "Look what I found—"
And then the tide pulls sand

And shark back in. The gray corpse rolls then stalls.
Its pink mouth fills
With water; slipper shells, bleached white,
Float up and surround it,

While you sit on a boulder, winding cord,
Yard after yard
Around the stick that steers the kite.
A few more hours till night;

Hunched over us, the cliff half-dressed in brush,
Scarred pines and trash.
An automated light; a few
Yards back, its spire in view,

A real lighthouse: the original,
Museum-still,
The green park's centerpiece…He walks
Over the slicked-down rocks,

Slips once, regains his balance Now you're done.
We watch you run
Until wind takes the kite, until
The dragon's face looks small,

A yellow grimace swallowed by the milk-
White sky. The silk
Unravels quickly now. I stand
Close, watching cord unwind;

The kite, still rising, flees the sea, the cliff—
Not fast enough.
You jerk the wire, regain control.
The wind's so loud we yell.

My father stares up, laughing, "Can I try?"
You smile at me.
Later, we'll walk up wooden stairs
Endless and warped; I'll pause

To let him rest. You'll rush ahead and wait
For us. Not yet.
He'll slump but catch his breath. And when
I squeeze his hand again,

I'll feel his dead weight lift then disappear.
He'll rise and hear
The gulls above the breaking waves
Freed from their hidden lives.

The shark, useless below, will wash ashore
Hour after hour.
And when we reach the top, where tall
Shrubs bend to form a wall,

I'll push each branch aside or break it off,
Sick of this cliff,
The whitewashed lighthouse and the park,
The lamp that doesn't work,

This gate tangled with brush I'll tear away—
You'll start to cry
As if you'd seen us at our worst,
But I will kiss you first.

ON TOUR WITH THE
GLENN MILLER ORCHESTRA

For Carmine, on his birthday

He "dreams a lot" these days, my father says,
Meaning that he recalls his dreams, this time
Lifting the horn he doesn't even play,
Still waiting for his cue; and when he sees
The bandleader's baton raised once again
As in the days before the War, the flight
That took him far from home, beyond the storm
And radio waves, the static and a sky
Gone black, the old man stands, presses the valves,
And out comes *Stardust*, this his favorite song
That's always failed him on accordion
(Self-taught, diatonic), but in the dream
"It's not so hard," he says, brass over woodwinds
Rising gracefully. The stars at last.

ARRIVAL

Over Boston's Logan Airport, October 1994

Flying above the Northeast corridor,
I'm seated behind the wing where if the plane
Tips just right, what looks like the negative
Of some lost world appears: black holes suggest
Its landscapes. Cities slide past, etched in light,
In bright lines purified of all detail,
Beyond the jet's white noise. By day this blackness
Takes on shade and color, but tonight
The world consists of gold lines bearing stars
That glide at different speeds till they dead-end
And disappear, or pass beyond what's seen
To what is not: those hidden, unlit roads.
I peer out through scratched glass. Mild turbulence.
The wing swings up to block my view again.

A clear night. Like the one we left the house,
Your visit home near over: hours on guard,
Sharp words in Sign...You watched black water break
And flicker along the shore where couples parked,
Or glanced up casually. I turned as well,
Startled to see the jet descending fast
Toward us, toward Logan Airport—you laughed,
Silenced as that vast body blocked the sky,
Its wing-lights flashing: clear insignia,
Deafening turbines, slate-gray steel doors
Parting as landing gear swung from each hatch—
All these you'd known from childhood—while we walked
Still further along the shore. Kids ran ahead
To stand beneath each huge jet that swept past—

—And now I'm *on* that jet but can't pick out
The shoreline of South Boston from the scrawl
Of blinking lights, reflections whirling in
Deep pools of darkness. Now the pilot's voice
Breaks in to say—all noise. How can I land
Here once more, in *your* city, still cut off
From you by choice? I think of all we planned,
All that we *knew* would happen, that in some
Dark miracle I cannot comprehend,
Became this new life, this transfigured end
I cannot see. Whatever guides us now,
The blue lights of the runway rise up from
This city of your past. Soon, now, I'll land—
Begin again. These words I understand.

DISCOVERY

Before the Challenger *memorial service, September 1988*

First flight after disaster. Nothing moves
Except with grace, weightless beyond the glass,
Across a blue, bright ocean. Earth persists,
Its white clouds luminous, while here in space,
Unfastened, you turn slowly, heels to head,
Clipboard in hand, reading. What will you say?
Dear friends, your loss has freed us to begin
*Anew with confidence...*No, that's not right.
Lost moon and rubble, everything that moves,
All dangers no one can anticipate,
Dead still and silent stars so far away
That to behold them is to mourn their loss,
What's missing these last hours before the broadcast?
You weren't the first, and you won't be the last.

NOTES

"Losing Ourselves" owes a debt to Sven Birkerts'
"Losing Ourselves in Biography," *Harper's*, March
1995.

"Randall and Weldon in New York" adapts material
from William Pritchard's *Randall Jarrell: A Literary
Life*, as well as source material contained in Robert
Knoll's *Weldon Kees and the Midcentury Generation:
Letters 1935-1955.*

"Legacy" imitates Robert Herrick's use of iambic
monometer in "Upon His Departure Hence," each
foot of which, according to *The Norton Anthology of
Poetry*, "suggests to the eye the narrow inscription of a
gravestone."

"Discovery" makes use of Malcolm Gladwell's
"Blowup," *The New Yorker*, January 22, 1996.

Ned Balbo grew up on Long Island, New York and holds degrees from Vassar College, the Writing Seminars at Johns Hopkins, and the University of Iowa Writers' Workshop. A Pushcart Prize nominee, he has published poems in *American Poetry Review, Antioch Review, The Formalist, The Quarterly, Santa Barbara Review* and elsewhere; he is the recipient of a grant from the Maryland State Arts Council and winner of *The Lyric*'s quarterly and Virginia prizes. His work includes the narration text for the Miramax release *Microcosmos,* as well as reviews for *art journal* and *Verse.* He teaches at Loyola College in Baltimore and works as an academic dean for the Johns Hopkins Center for Talented Youth.